It's fu Creepy Spooks

Mark Bergin

Author:
Mark Bergin was born in Hastings, England. He has Illustrated an award winning series and written over twenty books. He has done many book designs, layouts and storyboards in many styles including cartoon for numerous books, posters and adverts. He lives in Bexhill-on-sea with his wife and three children.

Editorial Assistant:
Victoria England

HOW TO USE THIS BOOK:
Start by following the numbered splats on the left hand page. These steps will ask you to add some lines to your drawing. The new lines are always drawn in red so you can see how the drawing builds from step to step. Read the 'You can do it!' splats to learn about drawing and shading techniques you can use.

Published in Great Britain in MMXII by
Scribblers, a division of Book House
25 Marlborough Place, Brighton BN1 1UB
www.salariya.com
www.book-house.co.uk

ISBN-13: 978-1-908177-59-9

1 3 5 7 9 8 6 4 2

A CIP catalogue record for this book is available from the British Library.

Printed and bound in China.

PAPER FROM
SUSTAINABLE
FORESTS

Visit our website at **www.book-house.co.uk** or go to **www.salariya.com** for **free** electronic versions of:
You Wouldn't Want to be an Egyptian Mummy!
You Wouldn't Want to be a Roman Gladiator!
You Wouldn't Want to be a Polar Explorer!
You Wouldn't Want to Sail on a 19th-Century Whaling Ship!

Visit our Bookhouse 100 channel to see Mark Bergin doing step by step illustrations:

www.youtube.com/user/BookHouse100

Contents

Bat

1 Start with the head shape.

2 Add angry eyes and a mouth with fangs.

3 Draw in two pointed ears.

4 Add two wings.

splat-a-fact
Bats are the only mammals that can really fly.

you can do it!
Use a felt-tip for the lines and then add colour with watercolour paints. Dab on more colour with a sponge to add texture.

5 Draw in two legs and feet.

4

Witch

splat-a-fact

Witches make potions in their cauldrons and cast magic spells.

1 Start with this shape for the head and hat.

2 Draw in the peak of the witch's hat. Add the warty nose, mouth, teeth and angry eyes.

3 Add hair.

you can do it!
Use wax crayons to create swirly textures and paint over it with watercolour paint.

4 Draw in the body and the feet.

5 Add the arms, hands and a potion bottle.

Dragon

1 Start with a circle for the body.

2 Draw in this head shape.

3 Add angry eyes, ears, nostrils and sharp teeth.

splat-a-fact
Gargoyles scare off evil spirits.

4 Draw in two front legs. and one back leg.

you can do it!
Use coloured pencils. Put textured surfaces under your paper to create interesting effects.

5 Add a wing and a pointed tail.

Monster

1 Start with a box-shaped head.

Add ears, hair, stitches and bolts on the neck.

2 Draw in the eyes, nose and mouth.

4 Add the body. Draw a curved line and button for his jacket.

you can do it!

Use oil pastels, and smudge them with your finger. Use a felt-tip for the lines.

5 Draw in the arms with a circle for each hand.

6 Add legs and feet. and ragged trousers.

10

Ghost

1 Cut out a wavy shape for the body. Stick down.

2 Draw in a mouth and add two dots for the eyes.

splat-a-fact
Ghosts haunt old, spooky houses and come out at night.

MAKE SURE YOU GET AN ADULT TO HELP YOU WHEN USING SCISSORS!

3 Cut out two waving arms. Stick down.

Igor

2 Add two dots for the eyes. Draw in a bandage, a nose, ears, mouth and teeth.

1 Start with an oval shape for the head. Add tufts of hair.

3 Draw a circle for the body and a belt.

4 Add the arms with ragged sleeves.

you can do it!

Use brown felt-tip for the lines and colour felt-tips to colour in.

5 Draw in the legs and feet. Add trousers with ragged edges and a hole in them.

14

Mummy

1 Start with an oval for the head and dots for eyes.

2 Add bandages and a dot for the mouth.

3 Draw an oval for the body.

4 Add the arms.

5 Draw in two legs.

6 Draw in the mummy's bandages.

splat-a-fact
Mummies are wrapped in bandages and live in tombs.

you can do it!
Use wax crayons to create textures and paint over it with watercolour paint. Use felt-tip for the lines.

16

Scarecrow

You can do it!
Use a felt-tip for the lines and watercolour paints for colour. Add ink to the paint while it is still wet for added interest.

1 Start with an oval for the head. Draw a line through the middle.

2 Add eyes, a nose, a jagged mouth and a stalk.

3 Draw in curved lines.

4 Draw in a jacket, belt and frayed trousers. Add spiky straw feet.

Splat-a-fact
Scary faces are carved into pumpkins on Halloween.

5 Add two arms and straw hands.

19

Vampire

1 Start with a circle for the head and add two ears.

2 Draw in a nose, a mouth, fangs and dots for the eyes. Add eyebrows and hair.

3 Draw in the body and arms. Add collar and necklace detail.

4 Draw in the jacket and add a cape.

5 Add legs and feet.

you can do it!

Use a felt-tip for the lines and coloured pencil to colour in using scribbly marks.

21

Werewolf

you can do it!
Use coloured pastel pencils and smudge the colours with your finger. Draw the lines with felt-tip.

1 Start with this head shape.

2 Draw two angry eyes and nostrils. Add sharp teeth.

3 Add two front legs with furry paws.

4 Draw the back legs and bushy tail. Add a belt.

Splat-a-fact
Werewolves howl at the full moon.

22

23

Witch on broomstick

1 Start with the witch's face. Draw a line for the hat.

2 Add the pointed hat.

3 Draw in angry eyes, a mouth and teeth. Add warts and hair.

Splat-a-fact
Witches fly through the night on broomsticks.

4 Draw in the witch's tunic. Add arms and feet.

you can do it!
Draw the outlines in black felt tip. Colour in with coloured pencils.

5 Add a broomstick.

24

Witch's cat

3 Add a pointy hat and whiskers.

1 Start with an oval for the head. Add the chin.

2 Draw in the eyes, nose and mouth.

4 Draw in two overlapping ovals for the cat's body.

5 Add back and front legs and a curved tail.

26

Wizard

MAKE SURE YOU GET AN ADULT TO HELP YOU WHEN USING SCISSORS!

1 Cut shapes for the head and hat. Stick down.

2 Cut a shape for the face and stick down. Add eyes and a mouth with felt-tip.

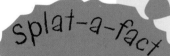

splat-a-fact

Wizards can turn people into frogs with magic spells.

3 Cut out a tunic shape and triangles for feet. Stick down.

you can do it!

As you cut out the shapes, stick them down on to coloured paper. Cut out simple shapes to make a bat and a frog.

4 Cut out the sleeves, hands and a wand and staff. Stick down.

skeleton

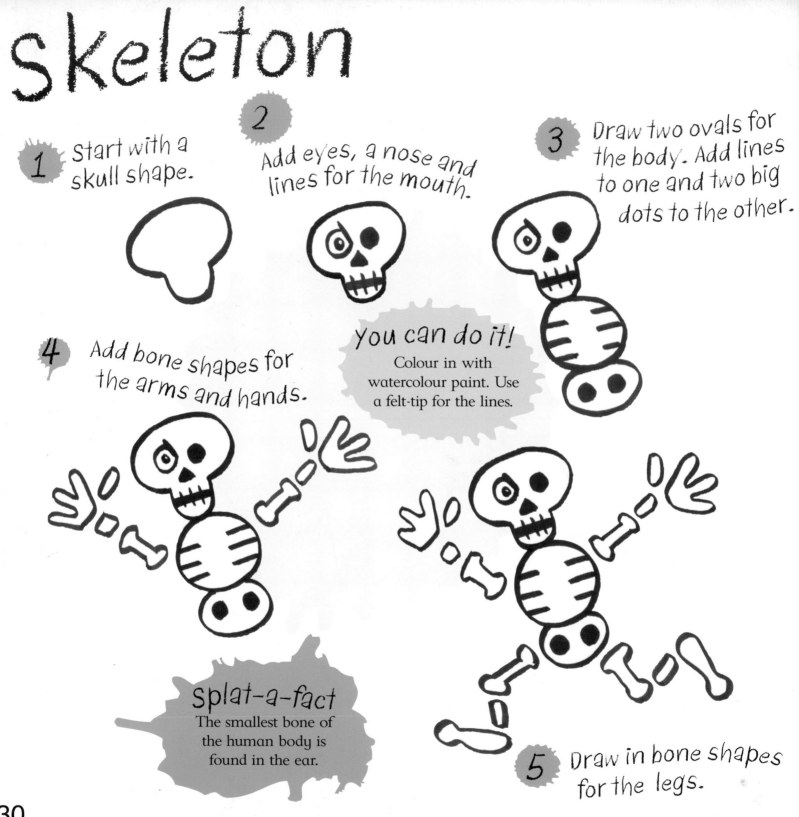

1. Start with a skull shape.

2. Add eyes, a nose and lines for the mouth.

3. Draw two ovals for the body. Add lines to one and two big dots to the other.

you can do it!
Colour in with watercolour paint. Use a felt-tip for the lines.

4. Add bone shapes for the arms and hands.

Splat-a-fact
The smallest bone of the human body is found in the ear.

5. Draw in bone shapes for the legs.

Index

www.salariya.com
where books come to life!

Download our free iPhone and iPad catalogue app. Search for Salariya or Book House

Available on the App Store

The Salariya Book Company is a UK-based independent publisher of books for children which sells both domestically and internationally. Through our imprints Book House, Scribblers and Scribo we are dedicated to publishing books with real child appeal, using innovative concepts, high-quality illustrations, informative writing and, above all, humour to captivate the minds of young people. With a mind for the environment, all of our books are printed on paper from sustainable forests. Click the links below to visit our imprints' websites, read our Book House Blog or dive into a world of free interactive web books from the best-selling 'You Wouldn't Want To Be...' series.

The Salariya Book Company,
25, Marlborough Place,
Brighton,
East Sussex
BN1 1UB
England
United Kingdom

Tel: 01273 603306
Fax: 01273 621619

rights - www.murray@salariya.com
press - jamie.pitman@salariya.com
editorial - stephen.haynes@salariya.com
managing director - david@salariya.com

twitter facebook flickr

Follow us on Facebook and Twitter

www.youtube.com/user/BookHouse100

Children's non-fiction and graphic novels

Scribblers
Bright Start

Scribo fiction

Fiction for children and teenagers

FREE WEB BOOK!
Free activities, puzzles and web books, with information about our books for babies, toddlers and pre-school

Four free web books

FREE WEB BOOKS!

THE BOOK HOUSE BLOG

The Book House blog - competitions, giveaways and current news